The Citizen's Guide to Mediation and Arbitration

What Every American Should Know About
Alternative Dispute Resolution

Doris Rebhorn Spies

THE CITIZEN'S GUIDE TO MEDIATION AND ARBITRATION
WHAT EVERY AMERICAN SHOULD KNOW ABOUT ALTERNATIVE DISPUTE RESOLUTION

Editorial Reviews by:
Spencer Sims, Julie Rael, Eldon Rebhorn, Dale Rebhorn, Sue Beaule and Kathy Fragnoli

Cover Art by Jeremy Sims

iUniverse books may be ordered through booksellers or by contacting:

iUniverse LLC
1663 Liberty Drive
Bloomington, IN 47403
www.iuniverse.com
1-800-Authors (1-800-288-4677)

ISBN: 978-1-4917-3337-0 (sc)
ISBN: 978-1-4917-3338-7 (e)

Library of Congress Control Number: 2014908301

Printed in the United States of America.

iUniverse rev. date: 07/02/2014

To order additional copies and/or bulk copies of this book, or to contact the author, visit our web site at: www.adrsupportguide.com

In memory of my mother, Marilyn, who always spoke up and took action to try to turn a wrong into a right.

Why I Wrote This Book

A few years ago I knew very little about mediation and arbitration; in fact, I thought mediation and arbitration were very similar processes used to resolve disputes. I never thought I would go through mediation or arbitration, even though I (like most Americans) had signed several contracts in my lifetime that included arbitration clauses. I did not understand what an "arbitration clause" meant in a contract.

But then a conflict escalated and I ended up personally experiencing both mediation and arbitration over a multi-year period. My experiences with these processes were challenging. But this is one of those situations where people say, "When life gives you lemons, make lemonade," and so I wrote this book to provide a support guide for others like me who find themselves going through (or considering) the alternative dispute resolution processes known as mediation and arbitration.

If I had known all of the information in this book, I could have potentially saved myself from years of conflict resolution problems and a whole lot of money and stress. If you are going through a conflict situation, I hope you will read through this book to consider all of your options. I learned many things the hard way, so I hope this book helps you learn the same information in an easy and proactive way.

Now, when I sign contracts, I check for arbitration clauses and I ask the contract owner to change any arbitration clauses to mediation clauses. This book will help explain why this is so important.

My gift from God is the ability to take complex subjects and write about them in a straightforward and practical way. I have written and published multiple books on other topics that are considered to be practical and informative guides by my readers. So now that I have been through this difficult but unique learning experience as a party to both mediation and arbitration, I believe I have a calling to write this book to increase the understanding of mediation and arbitration in the United States.

Because the laws and procedures pertaining to mediation and arbitration vary in countries around the world, this book pertains specifically to citizens of the USA and to USA mediation and arbitration laws and procedures.

There were so many things I learned too late to help my situation or to make a different choice. So I wrote this book to help others obtain information in time to make the best possible decisions if they are using mediation or arbitration to resolve their dispute.

The amazing thing is that there are few practical support resources designed to educate the public about alternative dispute resolution processes, even though virtually all adults in the United States have signed multiple legal agreements throughout their lives which contain a clause requiring them to mediate or arbitrate disputes.

Arbitration clauses can be found in most employment agreements, credit card contracts, healthcare agreements, financial agreements, home construction contracts, service provider contracts, insurance contracts and business contracts—if you have ever signed any of these documents, you are probably bound to an arbitration clause.

Often we sign contracts with arbitration clauses without understanding that we have just given away our civil right to a court hearing or to a judicial procedure in the public court system, which we are all already supporting by our tax dollars. *If you sign a contract with an arbitration clause, you are then legally bound to arbitrate any future disputes outside of the public court system, no matter the nature, the size or the scope of the dispute.* You have just agreed to waive your American right (and your tax-payer's right) to the use of the public court system if a dispute occurs with a vendor, a contractor, a doctor, an employer, or any party you contract with in a legal manner.

My vision for this book is to provide an easy-to-read resource to enhance your knowledge about mediation and arbitration so you can discuss your legal dispute from a more informed perspective. Anyone who is considering (or who is currently in) a legal dispute should be an educated participant in the process. My previous ignorance about mediation and arbitration placed me in a weak position and I did not always make informed decisions during my business dispute resolution process. After reading this book, you will be in a better position to discuss options with your attorney and to make more informed decisions.

This is not a legal manuscript. This book provides information—not legal advice. Consult your attorney for legal advice for your specific situation.

I am not an attorney. I am an American citizen and the author of other "how to" books. I am a regular person like you. But during my years of experience going through mediation, arbitration, and litigation, I learned a significant amount of information, and I am sharing the knowledge I learned from my experience with you. This book has also been reviewed by legal experts for technical accuracy, and I have included case law examples and internet resources for you to refer to as you read this book.

This book reflects current mediation procedures, current arbitration law and case law examples that exist at the time of publication. It is important to work with your attorney to learn about any new laws or new case law decisions that may affect your situation.

I entered into mediation and arbitration with no clue about what I was doing or how important my choices were as I went through these processes. It is my sincere wish that this book will help you make better decisions when you sign contracts, or that it will be a helpful support guide for you if you are currently in a dispute resolution process.

Doris

How to Use This Book

Information about mediation and arbitration is presented in separate chapters, because you may only be using one of these alternative dispute resolution (ADR) processes. This enables you to focus only on the chapters that apply to your situation. However, if you are considering arbitration but you haven't agreed to arbitration yet, read the chapters on mediation to help you decide if mediation might be a preferred conflict resolution method for you.

The content in this book is designed to inform and to educate. It is not designed to either support or refute the advantages and disadvantages of mediation or arbitration. Every road and every decision we take holds risks and benefits; therefore, both advantages and disadvantages of alternative dispute resolution options are presented in this book, to help American citizens weigh these perspectives as they work with their legal counsel to make decisions about their own dispute.

If you are using an attorney to help you with your mediation or arbitration (which is advisable), be sure to read *Chapter Two* to help you understand how to work with your attorney and how to keep your legal expenses under control as much as possible.

This book does not provide legal advice; it provides practical information about arbitration and mediation processes. Of course, it would be impossible to include every piece of advice or information in this book and still provide a usable and readable layperson's book on this topic, so again, please work closely with your attorney on your legal matter.

To contact the author of this book, or to order additional or bulk quantities of this book, locate the author's Contact Us page at **www.adrsupportguide.com.**

CONTENTS

Why I Wrote This Book vii

How to Use This Book ix

Chapter One: What is Alternative Dispute Resolution (ADR)? 1
    What is a Binding or a Non-Binding Process? 2
    What is Mediation? 3
    What is Arbitration? 4
    Comparing Mediation and Arbitration 5
    How Do We Decide on a Dispute Resolution Process? 6

Chapter Two: Understanding Legal Processes and Expenses 7
    Before You Jump Into Any Legal Process 8
    Working With Your Attorney 9
    Understanding Your Legal Expenses 10
    Monitoring Your Attorney Expenses 11
    Ethical and Unethical Attorney Billing Practices 12

Chapter Three: Keys to Successful Mediation 13
    How Do We Select a Mediator? 14
    Locating and Interviewing Potential Mediators 15
    What Ethics Should I Expect From My Mediator? 16
    What Mediation Decisions Will I Need to Make? 17
    How Do I Prepare for the Mediation Session? 18
    Additional Mediation Considerations 19
    Additional Words of Wisdom for a Successful Mediation 20
    Should a Mediator Also Serve as an Arbitrator? 21
    What Happens After Mediation? 22

Chapter Four: Arbitration Law and Procedures 23
    What is an Arbitration Clause? 24
    What Should I Do if I Receive an Arbitration Notice? 25
    What You Must Know About Arbitration 26
    A Summary of Facts to Consider Before You Decide to Arbitrate 27
    Arbitration Laws and the Arbitration Agreement 28
    Choosing an Arbitrator or an Arbitration Panel 29
    Ethics for Arbitrators 30
    Arbitration Process Steps 31
    Comparing Arbitration to Court System Procedures 32

Chapter Five: Avoiding Arbitration Problems *33*

    What if the Arbitrator Violates Our Arbitration Agreement? 34

    What if a Conflict of Interest is Discovered? 35

    What if the Arbitrator Demonstrates Bias or Misconduct? 36

    A Summary of Key Points About ADR 37

    Additional ADR Information Resources 38

Glossary of ADR Terms 39

Acknowledgements 41

Chapter One

What is Alternative Dispute Resolution (ADR)?

Alternative dispute resolution (abbreviated as ADR) refers to private processes used by people who want assistance to resolve a conflict without using the public local, state or federal court system. **ADR refers to the range of private negotiation, mediation and arbitration business services that USA citizens can purchase to resolve a dispute.** This book explains the differences between these ADR options.

Mediation and arbitration have been around as long as there have been conflicts between people. For centuries, parties in conflict have asked others to help them resolve a conflict that they cannot resolve themselves. Of course, ADR processes have evolved over time. Most countries of the world have mediation and arbitration laws and services. This book pertains only to ADR procedures and law in the United States.

Why is the information in this book important to you? Most Americans sign documents with arbitration clauses without realizing what this means (I certainly had no idea before I went through arbitration myself). Virtually all Americans have signed <u>many</u> legal documents with mediation and/or arbitration clauses. These statements are often found in employment agreements, medical forms, financial and business contracts, service contracts, construction contracts, mortgage agreements and credit card contracts.

When you sign a contract with a **mediation clause**, you are agreeing to share the cost of mediation with the other party if the dispute can't be resolved without this assistance.

If you sign a legal document with an **arbitration clause**, you will be legally obligated to submit any future conflicts with the contract owner to arbitration. Additionally, you will be legally obligated to share the costs of arbitration (which could be thousands of dollars) and you have waived your American civil right to file a lawsuit within the public court system on the same topic of dispute.

Today, if a contract I am considering has an arbitration clause, I ask the contract owner to change it to a mediation clause. I have discovered that most contract owners are agreeable to this. As another option, cross out the arbitration clause and both parties can date and initial this contractual change. If a dispute does arise in the future, you and the other party can still decide *voluntarily* to submit the dispute to an arbitrator. But it is best to leave your options open in a contract, because you don't know what type of dispute might arise in the future.

Additionally, you can choose not to sign a contract with an arbitration clause at all, and simply not enter into a contractual agreement with the other party if they are not willing to change the arbitration clause.

> *There are advantages and disadvantages to using mediation or arbitration services, which are discussed in this book to help you make informed decisions.*

What is a Binding or a Non-Binding Process?

Mediation is typically a **non-binding** process, while arbitration typically results in a **binding decision**. *However, it is critical that you read the contract associated with your mediation or arbitration procedures to determine if you are entering into a non-binding or a binding process.*

Don't sign any legal document with a mediation or arbitration clause unless you are able to determine if you are entering into a binding or a non-binding process.

Mediation is *Typically* Non-Binding

Arbitration is *Typically* Binding

You will retain options to resolve the dispute, and the mediator does not make decisions for you.

A neutral party (the arbitrator) resolves the dispute for you, and both parties must comply with the arbitrator's decision.

- You are agreeing to voluntarily attempt to resolve the dispute with the other party, and to reach an agreement together without legal action.

- You retain the right to withdraw from the process if you are not able to reach an agreement with the other party. You also retain the right to a hearing with a judge and/or jury if the dispute can't be resolved in mediation.

- No one can force you to reach a decision or to make a decision for you in mediation; however, once you reach an agreement and sign a legal document describing the terms of your agreement, the agreement then becomes binding (i.e. you must comply with the agreement you have just signed).

- You are agreeing to submit your dispute to one or more arbitrators (decision-makers) who will act in the role of a judge, making a decision about the dispute that can't be changed.

- This decision cannot be overturned by anyone else, including a judge. It is possible to ask a court to "vacate" or dismiss a binding ruling, but this is *very* difficult to obtain and is only provided in very limited circumstances. Even if the arbitrator's decision is legally incorrect, the arbitrator's decision is binding.

- ***Once you begin a binding arbitration process,*** all parties are obligated to complete their contracted arbitration actions, so be sure that arbitration is the best solution for your conflict before signing an arbitration agreement.

What is Mediation?

There are two primary types of ADR—*mediation and arbitration*—but these are very different legal processes. A mediator helps two parties resolve their conflict through a facilitated process, rather than making decisions for them. An arbitrator makes a decision for the parties in dispute and the parties must comply with that decision.

Mediation is a non-binding facilitated process that is designed to help two parties resolve a dispute outside of a courtroom by assisting the parties to work collaboratively to negotiate an agreement to resolve the conflict.

- Mediation is facilitated by a neutral person who has been trained in negotiation and mediation processes; the mediator is paid to serve in an objective role in the mediation meeting.

- The mediator will help each party work in a cooperative way to negotiate solutions to resolve one or more disputes. A mediator may suggest potential resolution ideas but a mediator should not make any decisions for either party.

- If the parties are able to resolve the dispute, the mediator will create a Mediated Settlement Agreement (typically abbreviated **MSA**) for both parties to sign, which confirms the terms of their agreement.

   NOTE: Although the mediation process is non-binding, the MSA becomes a binding contract once it is signed, and the agreement finalizes the mediation process. Both parties are then legally obligated to comply with their MSA (unless the MSA becomes a rare impossible contract because an external change occurs after the contract is signed which legally prevents performance).

- If the parties are not able to reach a settlement agreement, one or both parties can "walk away" from the mediation. However, because this will likely cause significant legal expenses for both parties, both parties are usually motivated to reach an agreement.

- A mediator might also be a qualified attorney or a retired judge, but it is not the role of the mediator to provide legal advice to either party.

- Mediation is a confidential process for the participants; in other words, what is said in the mediation session stays in the mediation session, and cannot be used in any future legal proceedings. This enables the parties to discuss potential solutions in a safe environment.

What is Arbitration?

Although mediation and arbitration are both forms of alternative dispute resolution (ADR) that take place outside of a courtroom, *there are no other similarities between these two legal processes.* Arbitration is <u>not</u> an advanced form of mediation. Arbitration is <u>not</u> the "automatic" next step of mediation. While mediation is designed to be a collaborative and a non-binding process, arbitration is designed to mirror courtroom processes, and the arbitrator will make a binding decision for the parties.

When two parties bring their dispute to an arbitrator (or to a panel of multiple arbitrators) they will both present their side of the dispute. One party will be the **Plaintiff** (the one who makes the claim or dispute to be resolved) and the other party will be the **Defendant** (the one who defends their side of the dispute) during the arbitration process. Each party will present testimony to the arbitrator, and each side will be cross-examined (questioned) by the attorney of the other party.

The arbitration process may include typical legal processes that are often used before, during or after a civil court hearing, such as:

> **Arbitrators make a final and binding decision for the parties, after hearing testimony about the dispute and after reviewing exhibits from both parties.**

- **Depositions**—the process of obtaining recorded testimony under oath.

- **Discovery and/or Production**—the process of asking the other party to disclose information, documents or other items.

- **Interrogatories**—a list of questions the other party is required to answer prior to the arbitration hearing.

- **Position Papers**—documents stating the position each party is taking in the arbitration.

- **Exhibits**—documents and items that will be presented to the arbitrator as evidence during the arbitration hearing.

- **Reply Briefs**—documents that may be submitted after the arbitration hearing to provide additional information such as case law citations.

- **Witnesses**—individuals who are asked (or subpoenaed) to provide testimony at the arbitration hearing.

Although arbitration mirrors courtroom processes, the arbitrator is not a publicly elected judge (although some arbitrators are retired judges with a private arbitration business). Arbitrators are private persons or organizations providing arbitration conflict decision-making services, and one or both parties are required to pay for the arbitration services.

Arbitration is designed to be a faster and less expensive legal process to resolve conflicts, compared to the typical time and expense involved in the judicial system. The reality is that this may or may not be true for your situation; there are arbitration cases on record that have gone on for years and which took more time and more expense than a court case. However, if arbitration is property facilitated, and if your dispute is not complex, it might be the fastest and least expensive way to resolve your dispute (if there is no hope of resolving the conflict through mediation). *Consider all arbitration advantages and disadvantages before making this decision.*

Comparing Mediation and Arbitration

On the previous pages we've discussed mediation and arbitration, which are both private alternative dispute resolution business services purchased by individuals or groups to resolve disputes. The diagram below compares these two ADR services to provide more clarification.

Mediation	Arbitration
The parties are responsible for creating their own decisions and solution(s) with the aid of a mediator who serves as the mediation session facilitator.	The arbitrator will make a decision (called an award) for the parties to resolve the dispute.
Mediation is normally non-binding; both parties retain the option to "walk away" if a settlement can't be reached.	Arbitration is a binding process which results in a final decision; once an arbitration agreement is in effect, the parties must comply with the process and with the arbitrator's decision.
You do not give up your civil right to a hearing in the public court system when you agree to first try to mediate a solution to resolve the dispute.	Once you have signed a formal agreement to arbitrate, you have waived your right to a public civil court hearing on the same issue.
Mediation procedures are not similar to public court system procedures; the parties work with the mediator to try to reach an agreement that both parties can "live with".	Arbitration procedures are similar to public court procedures, with the arbitrator acting in the role of a judge. The parties typically use legal processes such as discovery, exhibits and hearings.
The parties determine who is responsible for mediation costs and attorney fees.	The arbitrator can rule that one party will pay the attorney fees of the other party, and the arbitrator can determine who pays the arbitration expenses.

How Do We Decide on a Dispute Resolution Process?

When a dispute arises between two parties, there are basically four ways to resolve the problem. The chart below identifies each of these conflict resolution choices, and the advantages and disadvantages of each.

Options	Key Advantage	Key Disadvantage
Option 1: The parties resolve the conflict <u>on their own</u>.	No attorney and legal expenses!	One or more parties may not be aware of their legal rights that pertain to the dispute.
Option 2: The parties pay for <u>mediation services</u> to help them resolve their own dispute.	An objective mediator can help parties in an emotional situation to negotiate and to quickly resolve the dispute at a minimal cost.	The parties may end up spending money on a mediation process that does not resolve the dispute, if one or both parties walk away from the mediation.
Option 3: The parties pay for <u>arbitration services</u> to make a decision for them regarding the dispute.	The dispute might be resolved in a faster and less expensive manner than a full court hearing.	The arbitrator will make a binding decision, and if one party does not agree with the decision or if the decision is not legally correct, the arbitrator's ruling still stands.
Option 4: The parties file formal litigation and <u>go to court</u> to resolve the dispute.	The court system has an appeals process if a party believes the judge's ruling is legally incorrect. Parties can also go to small claims court for minor disputes.	Court hearings typically take at least several months (or even multiple years) and will result in significant expenses (such as attorney expenses and court fees).

Note: If you have signed any type of contract with the other party, read the contract to determine the dispute resolution process that must be followed, and to determine if the contract has an arbitration clause. For example, if you have a dispute with a surgeon and you signed a contract prior to surgery that includes an arbitration clause, the surgeon or hospital can legally force you to arbitrate any disputes that could arise, and you can't choose the public court system to hear the dispute.

This is why it is so important to make sure you leave your dispute resolution options open in a contract before signing it. ***You are not legally required to sign a contract with an arbitration clause. No employer, doctor, company, vendor, entity or contractor can force you to sign a contract with an arbitration clause.*** Ask to have the arbitration clause changed to a mediation clause, which is non-binding and keeps your legal dispute options open.

Chapter Two

Understanding Legal Processes and Expenses

First of all, if you still have a choice to participate in ADR or to litigate your dispute in a public court, the most important advice this book can provide is to first **STOP** and consider the impact this decision will have on your family, your health and your finances. Ask yourself, "Is it worth it?" and "Can we resolve this dispute on our own, or can we just settle this and move forward?" My own business conflict not only affected my life for years, but the conflict significantly affected my loved ones as well.

Consider the toll this conflict could take on your life and on your family:

Financial Stress

The financial impact of any legal dispute process is typically thousands of dollars, at minimum. You could end up in debt, bankruptcy or worse.

Relationship Stress

Legal disputes will take time, attention, money and your focus away from the important relationships in your life. Your loved ones will feel the stress you feel.

Health Stress

Conflicts, legal expenses and legal actions cause significant stress that can impact your mental and physical health.

Before You Jump Into Any Legal Process . . .

Before moving forward with any type of legal dispute process, consider the following:

- Any type of litigation process will be expensive. At minimum, you will typically pay thousands of dollars to an attorney, to a mediator, to an arbitrator, and/or to the court system (for court fees)—the list is far more extensive than most people realize.

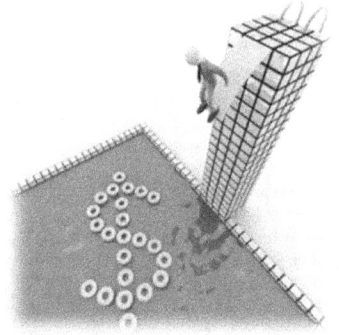

- Even if you win your case in arbitration or in court, it is very possible that you will never actually obtain a financial award; litigants with a judgment against them can file bankruptcy or submit appeals that can take years (and more money) to complete.

- An ADR or litigation process will impact your personal life and your job or business more than you can imagine. Even when you are trying to enjoy time with your family, or if you are on vacation, or if you have an important project at work, a stressful situation pertaining to your litigation can occur at any time, impacting your relationships, your work and your leisure time. In my own situation, a legal issue would suddenly come up during important times and events with my loved ones, and so I can tell you from personal experience that these are not the type of memories you want to create for your children.

- The litigation process can affect your physical and mental health, because conflict and legal processes are very stressful on a long-term basis.

- If you submit your dispute to an arbitrator or to a judge in a binding legal process, both parties lose control over their own situation. Binding legal decisions literally put your life path into the hands of someone who doesn't know you, and into the hands of someone who may or may not make the most accurate or even a legally compliant decision (arbitrators have been allowed by some courts to make decisions that are contrary to law). Are you sure a total stranger knows what is best for your situation?

- Any binding litigation process will require significant time and attention. Many people think that a legal dispute only involves a quick hearing in a courtroom. The truth is that any public court hearing can be preceded by months (or years) of other time-consuming legal processes. You may be asked to produce dozens or even thousands of documents. You may be deposed (required to answer questions under oath prior to a trial or hearing). Often there are multiple motions (court documents) filed in court prior to a court hearing. A very common strategy taken by an opposing litigant is to "bury" the other litigant in paperwork, motions, production requests, or interrogatories (questions to answer). These expensive processes will require you to take significant time away from your job or business, as well as time away from your family, your hobbies and your overall enjoyment of life.

Before you enter into a litigation process voluntarily, talk with your attorney about what to expect. Then talk with your family to hear their views on the situation and consider a non-binding mediation dispute resolution.

Working With Your Attorney

Be sure to choose an attorney with knowledge and experience with mediation and arbitration processes—**don't assume that all attorneys have these competencies!**

Although you are not required by law to use the services of an attorney before, during or after mediation or arbitration, it is <u>highly advisable</u> to have the aid of legal counsel who:

- Knows the law and will work to protect your legal rights before, during and after mediation or arbitration. Remember, it is not the job of a mediator or an arbitrator to advise you of your legal rights.

- Can serve as an objective person who is on your side (remember that a mediation or arbitration session will likely be an emotional experience for you).

- Can discuss your mediation goals with you before the mediation session, and provide legal advice to help you prepare for the mediation session.

- Will review the legal and binding document that is the result of a successful mediation (known as the MSA or Mediated Settlement Agreement); it is important to have an attorney review this document to identify any potential issues or changes that are needed before you sign the document, which will seal your agreements and obligations and create a binding settlement contract.

- Will help you prepare for an arbitration hearing and write the legal documentation that is typically required before and after the arbitration hearing.

- Will question the other party during an arbitration hearing to obtain testimony, and will assist you as you are being questioned in the arbitration hearing.

- Will assist you in completing any other legal processes, court filings or other paperwork that might precede or follow mediation or arbitration processes.

The only disadvantage of having an attorney work with you through the mediation process is that this can add additional expenses. If you can't afford an attorney to assist you during the mediation discussion, it is *highly advisable* to have an attorney review any resulting mediation written settlement contract before you sign it.

Typically the parties in conflict share the cost of the mediator, but each party is responsible for his or her own attorney fees.

It is not advisable at all to arbitrate a dispute without the aid of an attorney to represent you. You will likely find yourself completely overwhelmed with legal processes, methodology, terms and documents.

A lack of legal representation could cause you to become the losing party in arbitration.

Understanding Your Legal Expenses

Just as it is important to understand your consumer and legal rights for every other major purchase you make in your lifetime, it is very important to understand legal billing practices. Legal expenses can add up very quickly and you need to be <u>assertive</u> and <u>informed</u> about your legal bill. Don't assume that all attorneys operate in a fair and ethical manner, and don't assume that all attorneys use the same fee structures.

First, there are three basic attorney fee arrangements:

1. **Contingency Fee Agreement:** If it is expected that you are likely to receive a financial award or settlement in your case, an attorney may agree to work with you on a contingency fee basis. In this situation, you don't pay the attorney up front (or, you may be responsible for some legal fees, such as a court filing fee, so you need to make sure it is clear in your contract).

   However, if you win a financial award or settlement in a contingency case, your attorney will receive a percentage of this amount as his or her fee. A typical contingency fee may be 30%-50% of your financial award. Obviously the advantage of this arrangement is that you, as the litigant, have very little or no financial risk or expenses up front. The disadvantage is that you will need to forfeit a large amount of any legal award received to your attorney.

   In many situations, a contingency fee arrangement will not be offered to you as an option by the law firm. You should also be aware that litigants often have to pay taxes on the award percentage amount that the attorney receives, because the IRS sees this amount as part of your overall financial award.

2. **Hourly Fee Agreement:** In this situation, you are responsible for paying an hourly rate to all attorneys, paralegals and legal assistants who work on your case. Normally you will pay the legal firm a retainer, which is an amount of money you will pay up front. The legal firm will place the retainer into a bank account, to draw from as they work on your case. Typical attorney fees run from $300—$600 an hour, so as you can imagine, this can add up quickly. It is your right to know how much time your attorney is spending on your case on a regular basis, so you should receive a detailed monthly bill, but you can request more frequent communications and billing information to monitor your legal expenses.

3. **Flat Fee Arrangement:** Some attorneys may take a case or provide a specific service using a flat fee arrangement, which means they tell you in advance the amount you will pay for one or more specific services, rather than charging you on an hourly basis. A flat fee arrangement is most commonly used for standard legal services such as the preparation of a standard will, where the number of hours that will likely be required is known. Flat fee arrangements are not commonly used for court cases that could take months or years to complete.

If you are going through a mediation process, do not expect the mediator to order the other party to cover your attorney expenses; this would not be appropriate action for the mediator to do. Remember that the parties in mediation make the decisions regarding their own dispute resolution. **If you are going through an arbitration process,** the arbitrator can decide who is responsible for the legal expenses and for the arbitration fees associated with the case according to your arbitration agreement terms.

Monitoring Your Attorney Expenses

Even though it is expensive to have an attorney working with you during your mediation or arbitration, it could easily be much more expensive if you don't know your legal rights, or if your Mediated Settlement Agreement is not well written and it results in more legal disputes or other problems at a later date.

Here are some ideas to help keep your legal fees under control:

> **Make sure you have a written contract with your attorney that describes the specific services he or she will provide, the cost of these services and the hourly rates of anyone else who may work on your case.**

> **Ask the attorney to provide an estimate of the cost of his or her support in your ADR. Ask about potential factors or situations that would increase the cost of the ADR.**

> **You have a right to consult with multiple attorneys to find one that has a fee structure and style that is comfortable for you. Make sure the attorney will not charge you for your initial consultation.**

> **Find out how (or if) your attorney "rolls up" hours worked. For example, if an attorney works on your case for 50 minutes, is that rolled up to 1 hour on the case?**

> **Very Important!**
>
> **If you are asked to provide a retainer (a pre-paid amount of money) to your attorney, require that your attorney notifies you immediately if (or when) the attorney's fees and expenses have exceeded this retainer amount, to avoid unexpected legal expenses that are over your budget.**

Ethical and Unethical Attorney Billing Practices

At one point in my challenging arbitration situation, I hired a new attorney and paid an $8,000 retainer to the firm to begin work on the case. Within one month, the attorney informed me that I now owed tens of thousands of dollars. I received no notice from the attorney that my retainer funds had been depleted and that more funds would be needed to continue work on the case. You must be diligent and careful when contracting with attorneys so this doesn't happen to you.

As with every type of business, most attorneys are knowledgeable, ethical and fair, but there are a few who unfortunately use unethical practices in their billing procedures. To protect yourself, you must review your attorney bills carefully, you must ask questions about an attorney's billing practices, and you must analyze your contract with the firm. While it is certainly illegal for attorneys to charge for services that have not been rendered, there are some legal but unethical practices to watch for, as shown below.

Ethical Billing Practices	Unethical Billing Practices
Your bill should list every action performed as a separate line item. For example, if your attorney meets with you for one hour and then spends 30 minutes sending e-mails for your case, and a paralegal spends two hours researching case law about your case, each of these actions should be listed as a separate line item on your bill, with the individual amount of time spent by *each* person on *each* action.	**Do not accept "bulk billing" practices (also known as block billing or aggregate billing) in which actions are grouped together on your bill.** For example, it is not ethical for an attorney or law firm to list 3 hours of work for "e-mails, phone calls and research" as a general statement on your bill.
Your contract should define how billable time is "rounded up". Most attorneys have a minimum increment of time for each item billed; this minimum increment could be anywhere from .10 (one tenth of an hour, which is 6 minutes) to .25 (quarter-hour, or 15 minute increments). For example, if an attorney spends 8 minutes on a phone call with you, this might round up to .25 of an hour, which would be $100 for an attorney who charges $400 per hour.	**A law firm should disclose their minimum billing increment in their contract and they should follow this policy accurately. Bill padding or task padding are both unethical practices.** For example, if the minimum increment is .25 hours (15 minutes) but if everything you see on your bill is rounded up to a full hour, this is something you should pay attention to and inquire about.
Junior attorneys and paralegals who have a lower hourly rate should be handling more routine work. This practice will enable the more experienced (and higher priced) attorneys to spend time on the more complex aspects of your case. This is a good practice that can lower your expenses.	**Watch out for a significant amount of time spent by a junior attorney that is then "re-worked" by a senior attorney.** In this situation, you are paying for work that never produces anything for your case. In other words, you are paying to train the new attorney and you are paying for two attorneys.

Chapter Three

Keys to Successful Mediation

Remember, mediation is designed to be a collaborative process in which both parties work with an objective mediator who will assist the parties to reach a resolution on their own. Two parties in dispute should consider mediation when one or more of the following factors apply:

- The parties want to avoid the costs involved in a court litigation process.

- Both parties are motivated to achieve a settlement agreement and are willing to try to work to resolve the dispute together.

- Both parties have enough trust in the other party to comply with a Mediated Settlement Agreement (MSA) after each party signs the agreement.

- The parties want to retain a level of control over their own agreements and decisions, rather than having a judge or arbitrator make a decision for them; this may be especially important to parents who are trying to resolve a child custody dispute.

- The parties have tried unsuccessfully to negotiate a settlement on their own and they need the skills and experience of a trained mediator to help them achieve an agreement.

- The parties need to try to maintain a respectful relationship after the dispute is resolved which could be further damaged by court litigation or arbitration (as would be the case for divorcing parents or family members who own a business together).

- The parties want to avoid a lengthy court litigation process.

- The parties prefer a confidential discussion settlement approach rather than a public litigation procedure.

- The parties want to use mediation to finalize details that have not been resolved by a judge in a courtroom proceeding.

While it is certainly ideal if both parties can reach a resolution that each party considers a "win", the truth is that typically each party will gain things of importance and each party will need to give up things of importance in order to reach a settlement. Usually neither party is completely happy with the settlement, but both parties understand that a compromise is needed to resolve the conflict, to leave the dispute behind and to move forward with their lives without further stress and expense.

How Do We Select a Mediator?

To achieve a successful settlement in mediation, it is important for both parties to have a basic level of trust in the mediator. The parties should select a mediator who is skilled and experienced in conflict resolution, listening techniques, negotiation and mediation processes. Both parties should agree on the selection of a neutral mediator.

To select a mediator:

- Ask the potential mediator to disclose any potential conflicts of interest in a written document; your mediator must be a neutral party who has no previous relationships or conflicts of interest concerning either party.

- Ask the mediator to provide information about his or her education, certifications, training, credentials and mediation experience. Ask which ADR organizations the mediator is associated with. **The fact is that there are no federal training or certification *requirements* for someone to start a mediation business, so you must ask these questions to learn about the mediator's qualifications.**

  NOTE: Some states have training requirements for court-appointed mediators, but don't assume that the judge appointed a mediator with these credentials. So if a court appoints a mediator for your case, check the mediator's credentials, and remember that mediation is recommended but voluntary (although the courts may not look favorably on you if you refuse to mediate before returning to the court system). Do some research and ask questions to find out if the appointed mediator has the required credentials for your state, and remember that you always have the right to choose your own mediator.

- Determine if you need a mediator with a special area of expertise, such as a divorce mediator or an intellectual property mediator.

- Interview more than one mediator to select a mediator both parties are comfortable working with to resolve the dispute.

- Ask the mediator to provide information about all costs, expenses and fees involved in all processes that would (or could) take place before, during and after the mediation session.

- The mediator should provide a written document to you that includes the pricing, the process and the procedures he or she will use in the mediation process; if the mediator can't provide this, go to a different mediator.

- Ask the mediator about his or her time availability to spend on your case and to hold a mediation session in the near future.

- If you are already working with an attorney, he or she may be able to recommend one or more mediators for you to interview.

Locating and Interviewing Potential Mediators

Directories and referral services for mediators are available. One Internet resource is **www.mediate.com**, which is a business that provides multiple mediation services such as mediator directories and information on the topic of mediation. You can also view the membership directory of the *Association for Conflict Resolution* (ACR) at **www.acrnet.org**.

Both parties in dispute are looking for a mediator they trust and feel comfortable working with. If it is difficult for the parties in dispute to agree on a mediator, they could both do some independent research and make a list of mediators they are comfortable working with and then exchange lists, to identify one or more mediators the parties are willing to select. The parties can then interview these mediators to make a final selection.

Ask about all of the services the mediator provides for the price quoted, and find out what additional services are available for additional charges. Ask the mediator to describe any and all services he or she can provide for you; for example, will the mediator write the Mediated Settlement Agreement for the parties? Will the mediator file any paperwork with the court, if applicable?

Also ask about mediation session cancellation policies, in case you and the other party are able to reach a settlement prior to mediation, or in case an emergency situation or illness requires the mediation session to be rescheduled.

Ask the mediator to provide references from attorneys who represented parties in previous cases with this mediator (they will not be able to provide references for previous clients due to the confidential nature of mediation).

What Ethics Should I Expect From My Mediator?

On this page we will discuss some highlights from the *Model Standards of Conduct for Mediators*. These Standards were written in 1994 and revised in 2005 by a joint committee that included members of the American Arbitration Association, the American Bar Association's Section of Dispute Resolution and the Association for Conflict Resolution. Additionally, in 2005 the Supreme Court approved ethical standards documented in *Ethical Guidelines for Mediators*. You are encouraged to view these documents which are easily found on the Internet. Here are some key points from the *Model Standards* that you should expect from your mediator:

- **A Self-Determination Process:** A mediator should conduct mediation based on the principle of party self-determination. What this means is that the mediator should not make any decisions for the parties, and the mediator should not force or coerce the parties into reaching an agreement. The mediator serves to assist with communication and negotiation to help the parties come to a voluntary settlement agreement.

- **Impartiality:** The mediator must be free of bias, prejudice or partiality; if you believe your mediator is not impartial or is not behaving in an impartial manner, you have a right to withdraw from the mediation process. The mediator should disclose any factors that could create a bias or a conflict of interest toward either party, and the parties then have a right to choose another mediator. The mediator should not serve in any other personal or professional role for either party at any time.

- **Competency:** The mediator should demonstrate competency in mediation processes and procedures; the processes he or she uses should be disclosed and discussed with you and provided in written format.

- **Confidentiality:** The mediator must maintain the confidentiality of the mediation discussions; the discussions that take place in a scheduled mediation session cannot be used in a future legal proceeding as testimony or evidence. The mediator should not have ex parte discussions (private conversations that are unknown to the other party) outside of the scheduled mediation session.

  NOTE: There is an exception to the confidentiality rule if an act of violence or domestic abuse is reported in the mediation session.

- **Time:** The mediator should be able to devote the time, focus and attention on the mediation process.

- **Fee Disclosure:** The mediator's fees should be stated up front and should be provided in writing to both parties. If the parties are not sharing the mediation expenses equally, the payment agreement should also be in writing, and the mediator should not show preference to any party based on this fee arrangement.

What Mediation Decisions Will I Need to Make?

Before your mediation session, you will need to make decisions about your mediation process, and you will want to put careful thought into these decisions.

Decision: Should I be represented by an attorney at the mediation session?

Read *Chapter Two* of this book to learn about the importance of working with an attorney before, during and/or after a mediation session. Representation by an attorney at a mediation session is optional. However, it is important to remember that the mediator's job is not to provide you with legal advice, so many people do choose representation by an attorney before, during, and/or after the mediation session.

Before a mediation session, an attorney can help you prepare for the mediation by discussing what is most important to you, and by discussing options with you. **During** the mediation session, an attorney can provide legal advice and additional ideas to reach a settlement. **After** the mediation session, it is highly recommended to have an attorney review the written settlement agreement to ensure the document accurately represents the agreement you reached in the mediation session, and that the document won't cause you to unfairly lose legal rights or create new legal problems for you.

Decision: Should we all meet in the same room (the other party, the mediator and any attorneys) during the mediation session?

Some mediators will suggest that the parties meet in separate rooms to discuss mediation options, in order to reduce the emotional level of the mediation session. The advantage of this approach is that it will likely reduce the emotional state of the meeting. A disadvantage of this method is that future misunderstandings about the mediation agreement terms could occur, because the parties were not able to hear what the other party said directly in the mediation; in this situation, the parties are dependent on the mediator to move back and forth between two rooms to accurately convey newly proposed settlement terms. If you do mediate in separate rooms, it is even more critical to review every detail of the terms in your Mediated Settlement Agreement. Talk with your mediator about these options, but remember that the choice is up to you.

Decision: Should any of the parties participate virtually in the mediation session?

In today's world, virtual meetings that eliminate the need for travel are commonplace. Therefore, when the parties involved in the dispute are located in different geographic locations, it may be appropriate to schedule a virtual mediation session. However, in some situations, today's virtual meeting tools will not create an ideal situation for the parties to listen to each other and to reach a dispute resolution. Talk with your mediator and attorney about these options.

Decision: Who will pay for the mediation costs, attorney fees and other expenses?

Agree with the other party about how the mediation expenses will be handled; for example, will the parties split the mediation costs? Will each party be responsible for their own attorney fees, or will one party take on more than 50% of these expenses? The parties in mediation can make their own decisions about how the mediator is paid.

How Do I Prepare for the Mediation Session?

The mediation session is designed to help you make one or more important decisions that will affect your life and potentially the lives of others affected by your decisions. You have invested your emotions, money and time in this dispute resolution process. Therefore, it is important to ensure you are as prepared as possible for the mediation session.

Consider: Do I need to obtain any counseling prior to the mediation session to help me deal with my emotions and stress pertaining to the dispute?

It is important to know that a mediator does not serve as a counselor or as a psychologist. While a mediator understands the emotions involved in the dispute, the mediator's goal is to help the parties reach an agreement, and not to provide counseling in the mediation session.

Therefore, for many people it is helpful to obtain counseling prior to the mediation to help them deal with the anxiety and stress of the conflict situation. A counselor can also help an individual think realistically and more objectively about the situation and the emotional impact to other parties who may be affected by the mediation agreement.

Consider: Do I know all of the issues that the other party will be interested in discussing at the mediation?

If desired, each party can provide a "pre-mediation" document to the other party prior to the mediation meeting, listing all points of dispute that will be discussed in the session. This will help each party prepare for the meeting, and this document can save time in the mediation session (which could also save money). Knowing the disputes to be resolved in mediation can also help prevent new conflicts from occurring in the meeting.

Consider: Do I have all of the documentation and information that I might need to refer to in the mediation session?

Gather together any documents, books, information and reference data that you may want to have with you for reference in the mediation session. If applicable, assign values to assets and to debts that will be discussed in the mediation.

You may also need documents such as business agreements, tax filings, or appraisal documents for reference in the mediation. In some situations, you may also need to bring testimonies, affidavits or documentation from experts or witnesses to the mediation session.

Additional Mediation Considerations

Consider: What assets or issues would I be willing to negotiate in mediation and what (if any) items are not negotiable points for me?

Prior to the mediation meeting, spend some time thinking about what is most important to you. Because you will likely be experiencing some emotion during the mediation session, it is a good idea to write down your thoughts on paper so you can refer to them as needed during the session. This will help you to think through the points of negotiation when you are in a calmer state of mind, and it will help to prevent either party from forgetting important points or issues during the mediation meeting.

Consider: Who will attend the mediation session?

Each party should communicate with the other party to provide the names and roles of any party who will be attending the mediation session (such as attorneys, experts, witnesses or an insurance representative) prior to the mediation meeting.

Consider: What will be the agenda of the mediation session? What procedures will we follow throughout the day? What action will the mediator take if one or both parties become too emotional to successfully continue the mediation, or if the parties reach a stalemate?

Be sure you have a written document that defines these procedures prior to the mediation session, and ensure that both parties agree with these procedures. It is important to agree on these processes ahead of time, while all parties are in a more objective state of mind. Then, both parties are ready to follow these procedures if a conflict escalates.

Also clarify the starting and ending times and the location of the mediation session; this is especially important if one or more parties must travel some distance to attend the mediation. The mediator can advise you regarding the amount of time to schedule for the mediation.

The mediator should provide a mediation agreement that includes these processes and defines the roles, responsibilities and ethics of all parties involved in the mediation. Make sure the mediation agreement states that the mediation is a voluntary process, and that any and all discussions and documents presented in the mediation session will remain confidential. The only exception to this confidentiality requirement pertains to a situation in which some type of abuse or other previously unknown criminal action is disclosed during the mediation.

Additional Words of Wisdom for a Successful Mediation

It is important to remember that if you and your opposing party choose to participate in mediation, you will both need to have a mindset of working towards solutions, in order to avoid spending time and money on a dispute method that does not result in a resolution. Here are some additional "Words of Wisdom" to help achieve a successful mediation:

- **Make sure that both parties are ready for mediation.** Don't schedule a mediation session too quickly on the calendar—one or both parties might need more time to handle their emotions about the conflict, and/or to prepare for the mediation to increase the chance for success.

- **Make sure Ground Rules will be in place during the mediation session.** Ask the mediator what techniques he or she uses when 1) emotions escalate, or 2) when the parties seem to be in a stalemate, or 3) when the parties have stopped listening to each other. If the mediator cannot provide this information, you may want to find another mediator, or you and the other party will need to identify your own methods to employ if or when these circumstances occur.

- **If both parties reach a settlement in the mediation session, the resulting Mediated Settlement Agreement should include due dates and responsibilities that each party must comply with to follow through with each agreed-upon action**; be specific about deadlines and expectations to avoid new conflicts after the mediation session.

- Some mediators add an arbitration clause to the Mediated Settlement Agreement, so that if any further disputes occur, the parties would then arbitrate those disputes, ***but this is not at all recommended.*** Remember that signing any legal document with an arbitration clause removes your right to litigate the dispute in the public court system, so leave your options open and don't include an arbitration clause in your Mediated Settlement Agreement.

Should a Mediator Also Serve as an Arbitrator?

The short answer to this question is no—a mediator should <u>not</u> serve as an arbitrator for the same parties and/or for the same dispute. This might be confusing because mediators often also provide arbitration services as part of their business model; this is a very common practice and it is logical for an ADR firm to provide both ADR services.

> **A mediator should never serve as mediator and as an arbitrator for the same parties after hearing information and negotiations about the dispute in a mediation session. After hearing this information, it is impossible to know whether or not a mediator can still be neutral (objective), which is a requirement for an arbitrator.**
>
> **The parties in non-binding mediation should feel free to speak openly to create a settlement agreement without fear of providing information that could be used later in a binding arbitration decision. After hearing mediation disclosures, the mediator can no longer serve as a neutral person in any future disputes between the parties.**

Don't agree to a "Med-Arb" (Mediation-Arbitration) process in which the parties agree that the mediator can become an arbitrator and create a binding resolution for the parties if they are not able to reach a settlement in mediation, or if more disputes arise from the settlement agreement. *This can put you in a situation in which "mediator-turned-arbitrator" makes a binding decision for you after you have disclosed confidential information in a mediation session with this individual.*

Additionally, if your mediation session takes place with both parties in separate rooms, you have no idea what the other party said in the other room, which could bias the mediator if he or she becomes an arbitrator.

Finally, remember that mediators are prohibited from coercing or forcing parties into a settlement, so if the parties have agreed that the mediator can become an arbitrator if they don't agree, one or both parties might feel that they are being forced into a settlement, which is contrary to the purpose of mediation.

You may be told that the Med-Arb process is effective and efficient. But remember that every business likes to sell their clients more services, and remember that mediation and arbitration firms or individuals are businesses, so choose one dispute resolution service at a time and don't be sold into services you may not need or want.

What Happens After Mediation?

Many times mediation is successful—in other words, the parties are able to identify one or more ways to resolve their dispute and reach a settlement. Other times, one or both parties will "walk away" from the mediation and a settlement cannot be reached.

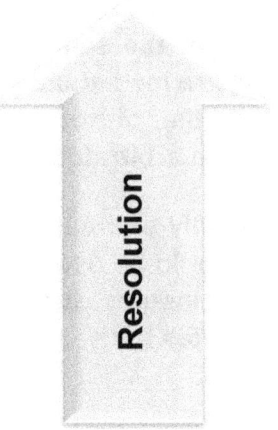

If your mediation is successful, the mediator will create a Mediated Settlement Agreement (MSA), which defines the terms of your agreement in a document. Read and review every word of this document, and make sure you have an attorney review the document before you sign it.

Be sure to put statements in your Agreement that define what will happen if a party fails to comply with the terms of the MSA. Remember that it is NOT advisable to state in your MSA that the parties will arbitrate any future disputes, because you don't know what can happen in the future, and you don't want to give up your civil rights.

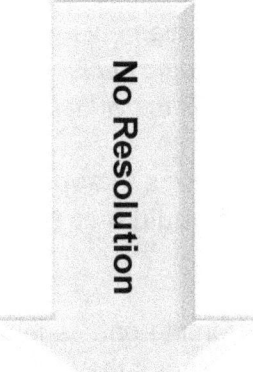

If your mediation was not successful, you will need to work with the other party to determine another way to resolve your differences. You might choose to mediate again with a different mediator, or to arbitrate the dispute, or to take your case to court.

Remember if you choose to arbitrate or take your case to court, you lose the control to reach a resolution together, and you will be submitting to a binding decision made by a judge OR by an arbitrator. Additionally, if you are not able to reach a settlement, the expenses, time and stress associated with the dispute will escalate.

Chapter Four

Arbitration Law and Procedures

When two parties in dispute hire an individual (or a group of arbitrators) to hear their case and to make a binding decision to resolve their dispute they are using the process of arbitration. Arbitration is a business service that can be contracted by and paid for by two parties. The parties in dispute are giving power to the arbitrator to make a legal decision for them and/or to make a financial award ruling of any amount. Often parties are already obligated to contract with an arbitrator to resolve their dispute because there was an arbitration clause in their original business contract, and the lesson here again is—don't sign contracts with arbitration clauses.

Although arbitration processes will vary based on the parties' written Arbitration Agreement, a basic model of arbitration is shown below:

The process begins when one or more of the following occurs . . .	The parties typically use the following steps to arbitrate their case . . .	The final steps typically include the following actions . . .
• Two parties are not able to resolve their dispute on their own and they voluntarily choose to arbitrate the dispute OR . . . • Two parties are not able to reach a settlement in mediation and they voluntarily decide to arbitrate OR . . . • Two parties in dispute begin the arbitration process to resolve a dispute due to an arbitration clause in a previously signed contract OR . . . • Two parties are ordered by a court to go to arbitration to enforce a contract with an arbitration clause.	• Each party obtains an attorney to assist with each step of the arbitration process. • The parties choose one or more arbitrators and sign an Arbitration Agreement that defines their arbitration procedures and deadlines. • The parties often participate in a discovery process to obtain pre-hearing information and documents from the other party. • The parties participate in a live Arbitration Hearing. • The parties provide any final documentation to the arbitrator as defined in their agreement.	• The arbitrator reviews the testimony, the arbitration exhibits and the documentation provided by both parties in the case. • The arbitrator writes a document that contains his or her decision about the case; this document is referred to as an award. • Depending on the terms of your arbitration contract, this award may designate one party to pay financial damages and legal expenses. • The arbitrator's award must then be confirmed by a public court judge before it is finalized.

What is an Arbitration Clause?

Most Americans are subject to multiple arbitration clauses in contracts they have signed without realizing the meaning of the arbitration clause. **An arbitration clause is a statement in a contract that requires you and the contract owner to submit any future disputes to an arbitrator to resolve the conflict.**

Arbitration clauses are often found in documents such as:

☑ **Credit Card Agreements**

☑ **Home Builder or Remodeling Contracts**

☑ **Mortgage or Loan Documents**

☑ **Divorce / Other Family Legal Documents**

☑ **Medical Forms and Physician Agreements**

☑ **Employment or Hiring Contracts**

☑ **Other Service Contracts, such as a Cable TV or Internet Provider**

When you sign a contract with an arbitration clause, you are . . .

. . . giving up your civil right to a court hearing, regardless of the nature of the dispute that may occur in the future.	. . . agreeing to help pay for the services of one or more arbitrators, in addition to the attorney fees you will incur if a dispute occurs.	. . . agreeing that you will arbitrate a dispute if the other party compels (forces) you to do so.

What can you do? Ask the contract owner to change the arbitration clause to a mediation clause. Inserting a mediation clause instead of an arbitration clause still demonstrates that you want to avoid expensive court litigation in the event of a dispute, but it does not waive your civil rights, because if you are not able to reach a mediation settlement, you can take the dispute to the public court system. Often, the contract owner will agree to make this change.

If the contract owner will not make the change from an arbitration clause to a mediation clause, you can choose to either sign the agreement, knowing that you are agreeing to an arbitration clause, or you can choose to take your business or your employment elsewhere. You can also cross out the arbitration clause, write that you don't agree with the clause, and sign and date this change, but the other party must be aware of the change when they sign the contract.

What Should I Do if I Receive an Arbitration Notice?

If you receive notification that another party has a dispute with you and is compelling you to arbitrate the dispute—***don't ignore this notification!*** If you ignore an arbitration notification, the arbitration hearing can take place without you, which would virtually guarantee an arbitration judgment against you. This judgment against you (called an award) could include multiple provisions for you to follow and it will likely include a financial judgment against you, and you would still be liable for arbitration costs. Contact an attorney who is experienced in arbitration if you receive an arbitration notice.

The actions listed below provide a general plan to take if you are being compelled to arbitrate:

- Read this book thoroughly to gain understanding of arbitration and to know more about your rights.

- Find an attorney who is experienced in arbitration law, and ask the attorney to review the original contract you signed with the party who is demanding arbitration. The attorney will review the original contract you signed to determine if the arbitration clause in the contract is viable.

- Next, your attorney can help you determine if there is a possibility of a settlement with the other party. Working towards a settlement will enable the parties to retain control of the situation, rather than submitting the dispute to an arbitrator.

- If you must submit to arbitration, your attorney can help you by making sure the arbitrator is experienced and neutral. Your attorney can also help you create an Arbitration Agreement which will define the arbitration procedures and document the specific powers of the arbitrator. The attorney can also represent you through the arbitration process and in an arbitration hearing.

NOTE: Choose an arbitrator who has not already served as an arbitrator for the other party on a previous case. Some businesses *use the same arbitrator on an ongoing basis* to resolve disputes with customers and other businesses, so you don't want an arbitrator who is interested in this type of ongoing business relationship with the other party.

What You **<u>Must</u>** Know About Arbitration

Before entering into an arbitration agreement, it is important to heed this quote from the United States Securities and Exchange Commission (the SEC):

When the arbitration is over, the decisions of the arbitrators are final and not subject to appeal. If you are unhappy with the result, you cannot go to court to try again.

When you enter into arbitration, you are agreeing that the arbitrator is able to:

- ☑ Make a final and binding decision to resolve a dispute

- ☑ Order one party to pay a financial award <u>of any amount</u> to the other party

- ☑ Enter a "reasonable amount" (i.e. any amount) in the arbitration award to be paid to the arbitrator for his or her services (or for an entire arbitration panel)

If you are on the winning side of an arbitration award, these aspects of arbitration are obviously beneficial to you. However, keep in mind that even if you win an arbitration award, you will still have to pay for attorney and court costs to confirm the arbitration award in court, and you'll probably have to pay a firm to help you collect the award, assuming the other party doesn't file for bankruptcy before you can complete these actions. If the other party files for bankruptcy, you will then need to pay an attorney to represent your claim in the bankruptcy.

Remember . . .

The decision of an arbitrator cannot be changed.

A court will never change the decision of an arbitrator, *even if the arbitrator has made errors or has ruled contrary to law.* An arbitrator is not even required by law to explain the logic or law used to determine the award (unless the parties' Arbitration Agreement requires this very specifically).

It is possible (but very rare) for an arbitration award to be <u>vacated</u> (nullified) in court for very specific and limited reasons, but it can never be changed. If an award is vacated, this means the courts have found the award to be invalid. However, when an award is vacated, the dispute remains unresolved, and the parties are "back at square one" after spending thousands of dollars and time on an arbitration that achieved nothing.

An example of the court's view that an arbitrator's decisions are not required to be rooted in the law is found in the case of *School City v. East Chicago Federation of Teachers*, 422 N.E.2d 656 (Ind. Ct. App. 1981), in which the court noted:

Where, as here, the agreement contains a broad arbitration clause courts have generally held that arbitrators are not bound by the principles of substantive law . . .

A Summary of Facts to Consider Before You Decide to Arbitrate

1. Once you sign a legal document with an arbitration clause, you have forever forfeited your civil right to either submit a dispute to mediation or to the public court system. You are now legally required to arbitrate any future disputes.

2. Once you begin arbitration, it is virtually impossible to stop the process unless both parties agree to do so or they reach a settlement. This is true regardless of any conflicts of interest or other problems that occur during the arbitration. For these reasons, choose an experienced, neutral and reputable arbitrator.

   Arbitrators are not required to have any specific training, education, experience or certifications, so check each arbitrator's credentials carefully.

3. Remember that you cannot appeal an arbitrator's decision to a higher court, as you can do when a decision is made by a public court system judge. It is possible to have an arbitration award vacated (nullified), but this is rare and <u>very</u> difficult to obtain. To view the legal requirements to modify or to vacate an arbitration award, see Sections 10, 11 and 12 of the *Federal Arbitration Act* on the Internet.

4. The courts have confirmed (finalized) arbitration awards that are contrary to law; arbitrators are not required to rule according to the law.

5. Your arbitration hearing will not be transcribed by a court reporter or stenographer unless you arrange for and pay for this service, but it is **critical** that you hire a reporter to create a written transcript of your arbitration hearing. If you fail to do so, the verbal testimony of the parties **under oath** during the arbitration hearing can never be reviewed again, nor can it be used to vacate an arbitration award if needed. If the other party makes a statement under oath that is not transcribed by a reporter, it is as if the statement *never existed.*

6. **An arbitrator can include any additional payment amount due to himself or herself in the arbitration award.** Be sure to ask the arbitrator about how this payment would be structured and calculated, and agree in writing with the other litigant(s) as to how this payment would be shared (or not) between the parties.

7. If you hire an arbitrator through a commercial arbitration association and you have any problems with the arbitration process, the association should assist you with these issues. However, you should be aware that there are no government or consumer protection agencies to help you if you experience problems in arbitration, even though arbitration is a business service.

8. Rather than hiring one arbitrator, you can hire a panel of arbitrators to hear your dispute to reduce the risk of empowering one person to make an arbitrary award.

9. Never include a broad arbitration clause in a contract (such as "all disputes will be arbitrated . . ."). This type of statement leaves you at risk to be compelled to arbitrate regardless of the type of dispute or the significance of the dispute.

10. Take the arbitration process <u>very</u> seriously—some people have a misperception that arbitration is an informal process, but a binding arbitration decision can affect your entire life. It is just as binding (if not more so, because it can't be overturned) as a judge's decision in a court of law. You will need to hire an attorney to represent you throughout the entire arbitration process.

Arbitration Laws and the Arbitration Agreement

Arbitration is governed by the terms of the arbitration clause in the original contract between the parties, and by federal law, state law and the legal processes defined by the arbitration firm and/or within your Arbitration Agreement. Be very careful with the procedures of your arbitration as outlined in your Arbitration Agreement; this contract will govern your arbitration process and provide the specific authority for an arbitrator to act.

You can review the **Federal Arbitration Act** on the Internet to learn about the laws that govern arbitration clauses and arbitration procedures.

Case law decisions also impact arbitration procedures. **For example, in some states judges have ruled that an arbitrator is permitted to make a ruling that is *contrary to law*,** while other states are less tolerant of arbitrators who demonstrate "manifest disregard of the law" in their awards. This issue was reviewed at the federal level in 2008 by the Supreme Court, in the case *Hall Street Associates, L.L.C. v. Mattel, Inc., 552 U.S. 576 (2008)*. The Court ruled that even if arbitrators made legal errors in their decisions, it is not the place of the courts to review or to change the arbitrator's decision.

How will your arbitration be governed?

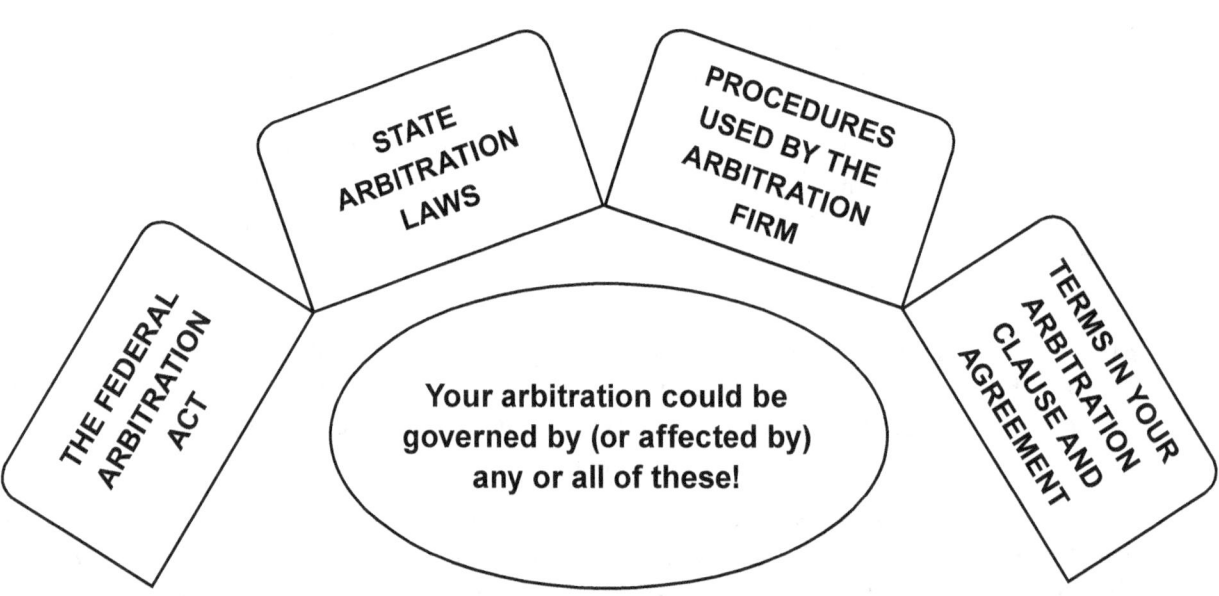

NOTE: *It is important to discuss and to document which law(s) will govern your own arbitration, and which courts will handle the post arbitration processes as needed. For example, will your arbitration be governed by the Federal Arbitration Act (FAA) or by state arbitration law? Which court will be used to handle any issues in your arbitration, and which public court system will confirm or vacate your arbitration award? These decisions should be documented in your Arbitration Agreement.*

Choosing an Arbitrator or an Arbitration Panel

Amazingly, even though arbitrators have immense power to make legally-binding decisions and to award parties unlimited financial rewards (some arbitrations have resulted in multi-million dollar awards) there are no federal training or certification requirements for arbitrators, and there is no consumer protection agency that oversees the business of arbitration. While most arbitrators do have legal backgrounds and credentials (many are attorneys or retired judges), it is important to know that literally anyone can be an arbitrator in the United States. ***What this means is that you <u>must</u> take responsibility to learn about the arbitrator's experience, education, credentials, and any potential conflicts of interest.***

Helpful Tips for Arbitrator Selection

- Large commercial arbitration firms do provide and require training for their arbitrators, so be sure to ask the firm about experience and education credentials they require for all arbitrators in their firm.

- Some parties create a specific process for arbitration selection; for example, each party can select one arbitrator and both parties must agree on one arbitrator, for a total panel of three arbitrators (or the two selected arbitrators can choose the third arbitrator). However, all arbitrators should sign a statement that they have no conflicts of interest in the case or in any relationships to either party in order to be able to serve on the panel.

- It bears repeating again here—an arbitration panel of three or more arbitrators is clearly more expensive, but this option can also help reduce errors or other problems that can occur with an individual arbitrator.

- Find out if the arbitrator is knowledgeable in the area of law that will pertain to your case. For example, if your dispute pertains to intellectual property, you will want an arbitrator (or a panel) with education and experience in this area of law. But if your dispute is a divorce or family law issue, an intellectual property arbitrator is obviously a poor choice.

- Another method of arbitrator selection is for both parties to submit the knowledge and credentials they require in an arbitrator (or in a panel) and provide this to an arbitration firm; the firm then selects arbitrators that meet these requirements.

- Don't choose an arbitrator who has had previous involvement with either party or with the case. For example, it is not advisable to select your previous mediator, a previous attorney or a previous arbitrator, because during any previous mediation, arbitration or litigation procedure, one or both parties have certainly disclosed information that may bias the arbitrator. Make sure the arbitrator does not have any previous or ongoing business arrangements with the other party.

- Ask potential arbitrators about their current caseload, to determine if the arbitrator will have sufficient time to devote enough focus and attention on your case, and to make a timely decision.

- Choose an arbitrator who is clear about the procedures and ethical code he or she will follow, and an arbitrator with extensive arbitration experience.

Ethics for Arbitrators

A document titled the **Code of Ethics for Arbitrators in Commercial Disputes** was originally prepared in 1977 (and revised in 2003) by a committee composed of members of the American Arbitration Association and the American Bar Association. This document provides clear behaviors, ethics and procedures to be used by arbitrators.

However, as of the printing of this book, the statements in the *Code of Ethics* document has not been used successfully to hold any arbitrator accountable for ethical behaviors in the public court system. So while this Code of Ethics document is a helpful reference for arbitrators and for parties who participate in arbitration, the statements are guidelines for arbitrators to follow and they do not currently rise to the level of law in the United States.

Some states also have a Code of Ethics for the arbitrations that take place in that state, so conduct an internet search pertaining specifically to your state on arbitration ethics.

Ask your arbitration firm about the ethical code of conduct that is expected for all arbitrators in the firm—you should receive a copy of this document.

Find out what action the firm takes if an arbitrator violates their code of conduct.

Ask the arbitrator or firm about cancellation policies if the arbitration process or arbitration hearing is halted because the parties reach a settlement on their own.

Make sure your arbitrator provides a document with his or her signature listing any potential conflicts of interest (or a document verifying he/she declares no conflicts of interest).

As of the printing of this book, there is pending legislation called the **Arbitration Fairness Act** which is sponsored by Senator Al Franken. If this Act is approved into law, it will help protect consumers from mandatory arbitration clauses which are found today in so many contracts and other legal documents.

Arbitration Process Steps

Arbitration procedures will vary due to the procedures of the arbitration firm and due to your Arbitration Agreement terms. If you contract with a large arbitration firm, the firm will already have a standard list of arbitration procedures. If you use a private arbitrator (such as an attorney or retired judge with an arbitration practice) you may have more flexibility in your arbitration procedures; *however, this flexibility to stray from standard arbitration procedures could also create problems in your arbitration.*

Below is a <u>basic</u> process flow for a typical arbitration:

Both parties agree to arbitrate a dispute. Or, only one party compels the other party to arbitrate a dispute due to an arbitration clause both parties signed in a previous contract.

The parties then select an arbitrator (or an arbitration panel) to hear their case and to make an award (decision) for them. The parties should have an Arbitration Agreement or contract that defines their arbitration procedures and the powers of the arbitrator.

If the parties have agreed to any pre-hearing discovery procedures (to gather information) these procedures will now begin. The parties may also have a pre-hearing meeting with the arbitrator to agree on the hearing dates and to discuss the process.

The parties will then present their case (testimony and exhibits) to the arbitrator in a hearing. Be sure to arrange for and pay a court reporter to create a legal transcript of your hearing.

After the hearing (or after completion of all actions of the parties) the arbitrator has a period of time (this should be defined in the Arbitration Agreement) to make an award, which is the arbitrator's written decision about the dispute.

After the arbitrator makes an award, the winning party has 1 year to have the award confirmed in the court system to validate the award. The other party can ask a court to vacate an award before it is confirmed, or by a 90-day deadline after the award is made, *whichever comes first.*

After a court confirms an arbitration award it becomes a judgment against the other party, who must then comply with the award. However, the losing party could appeal to a higher court to vacate the award (only in very specific situations such as a proven conflict of interest or fraud).

The winning party might also need to hire an attorney to collect the award, and/or to represent them in a bankruptcy court if the losing party cannot pay the award and must file bankruptcy.

Comparing Arbitration to Court System Procedures

In some ways, arbitration is similar to a court process, because two parties are submitting their grievances to a third party to make a decision about their dispute. But there are some very important differences between arbitration and judicial court processes, as shown below:

How are these processes similiar?

Both can include legal processes such as discovery, briefs, and depositions before, during and/or after the hearing on the dispute, and you will need an attorney to assist with these processes.

Both parties must take an oath to tell the truth in a court hearing and in an arbitration hearing; making false statements is perjury.

Both a judge and an arbitrator will hear and review evidence through testimony, briefs and exhibits, and then make a binding decision for the parties.

The parties in dispute are submitting their issue to be resolved by others, rather than retaining control over their own dispute resolution.

How are these processes different?

A decision of a judge or jury can be appealed and potentially overturned (changed) by a higher court; an arbitrator's award can't be changed by a higher court.

A judge is elected by and paid by the district he or she serves; an arbitrator is a private business person who is paid by the parties who are in dispute.

Many court hearings are documented by a court reporter who is paid by the district; in an arbitration, the parties must request and pay for a reporter or the hearing will not be recorded.

In court, your case may be decided by a jury or by a judge (this is a bench trial), but arbitration never involves a jury.

Chapter Five

Avoiding Arbitration Problems

I experienced challenging problems in my arbitration, which created difficulties for me, but which helped me to learn the information that is provided in this book. This chapter discusses some arbitration issues that could occur and ideas to potentially prevent these problems.

After the arbitrator has made an award (decision), a court must either confirm (finalize) or vacate (nullify) the award. However, it is very difficult to have an award vacated, as courts favor arbitration and the arbitration review process is very narrow and specific. The view of the courts is that bringing an arbitration dispute into the public court system destroys the purpose of arbitration, which is to settle disputes outside of a courtroom. If you think that ethical or contractual issues affected the result of your arbitration, <u>urgently</u> seek the advice of your attorney.

The winning party must motion to a court to confirm the award within a one-year time period or forfeit the award. A losing party must motion to a court to vacate the award within a 90-day time period, OR *before the court confirms the award, whichever comes first.* For example, if a motion to confirm the award is filed quickly, a court could confirm the award prior to the 90-day period if the other party fails to file a motion to vacate the award before the confirmation court hearing.

Remember that while arbitration is a legal process, it is also a business process; you are paying a private business person or an arbitration firm to settle a dispute for you. This makes arbitration very different from legal processes that are handled in the public court system.

As with every other business process, usually the arbitration procedure goes smoothly and the arbitrator reaches a timely and fair decision. The great majority of arbitrators are ethical and knowledgeable. However, just as every business experiences problems at times, the same can occur with your arbitration process.

While the ideas in this chapter can help prevent problems from occurring, it is also important to understand that it is impossible to create an Arbitration Agreement or process that will completely prevent problems from occurring during your arbitration. And because it is virtually impossible to stop an arbitration process once it has started, each decision you make about arbitrator selection and process is important.

If one of these problems does surface in your arbitration, there is a <u>small</u> chance that the arbitration award could be vacated (nullified) by a judge in the court system, although this will take even more time and expense.

What if the Arbitrator Violates Our Arbitration Agreement?

The courts have frequently referred to an arbitrator as a "creature of contract" because an arbitrator's power is defined and limited to the content of the parties' original arbitration clause and in the parties' Arbitration Agreement. An arbitrator exceeds this power if he or she makes an award after the deadline stated in the Agreement, or if an arbitrator makes an award that is outside of the scope of the Arbitration Agreement.

It is always best to prevent these types of problems from happening in the first place, so refer to the list below for prevention ideas:

1. Your Arbitration Agreement must state a specific deadline for the arbitrator to award. Additionally, the parties can add a statement that if the arbitrator does not make an award on or before this date, the parties agree that the arbitrator automatically loses jurisdiction after the award deadline, and the parties will seek a new arbitrator.

2. Make sure both parties sign and date the Arbitration Agreement with the type of clause described above. Additionally, make sure the Agreement spells out the decision(s) to be made by the arbitrator and exactly what the arbitrator is empowered to do, **and** what the arbitrator is not empowered to do. For example, if you want the arbitrator to explain the law and the logic behind his or her decision, you must specify this clearly in your Arbitration Agreement.

3. If you obtained your arbitrator through an association or firm, you should contact the firm to obtain assistance if the arbitrator does not award timely (but you still want to make sure your Arbitration Agreement follows items #1 and #2 listed above).

4. If the arbitrator fails to make an award by the Arbitration Agreement deadline, ask your attorney to send a formal written complaint to the other party and to the arbitrator (and to the arbitration firm, if applicable) to document the award delinquency. This is critical, because if you file a motion to vacate the award at a later date this documentation is required. You must file a complaint about an arbitration award delinquency **before** the arbitrator makes an award.

5. Another possibility is to ask the arbitrator to recuse himself or herself for failure to award timely or if he or she is not able to comply with your Arbitration Agreement.

If an arbitrator exceeds his or her power or fails to make a final award, there is a chance that either party could motion to a court to vacate (nullify) the award in the court system.

For more information review the *Federal Arbitration Act* (FAA) which provides that an arbitration award may be vacated when "the arbitrators exceeded their powers, or so imperfectly executed them that a mutual, final, and definite award upon the subject matter submitted was not made." 9 U.S.C. § 10(a)(4).

Review the case of *Baar v. Tigerman (1983)140 Cal. App. 3d 979 [189 Cal. Rptr. 834]* pertaining to an untimely award. Additionally, the *Code of Civil Procedure Section 1283.8* states: "The award shall be made within the time fixed therefore by the agreement . . . . The parties to the arbitration may extend the time either before or after the expiration thereof. A party to the arbitration waives the objection that an award was not made within the time required unless he gives the arbitrators written notice of his objection prior to the service of a signed copy of the award on him."

What if a Conflict of Interest is Discovered?

At some point in the arbitration process, you may discover a conflict of interest on the part of the arbitrator.

Like the problem of failing to make a timely award, this problem is difficult to correct once the arbitration begins, so it is best to try to prevent this issue from occurring in the first place. If you discover a conflict of interest during or after the arbitration, there is a small possibility that the award could be vacated (nullified in the court system). However, there are time limits to make a conflict of interest claim (90 days or less in some situations), and the courts would need to view the conflict of interest as being a significant matter that affected your arbitration process or award, which is difficult to demonstrate.

Ideas to prevent this problem (some of which have been discussed in earlier chapters) include the following:

State in your signed Arbitration Agreement that the arbitrator will lose his or her jurisdiction and authority to make an award in the case if a previously undisclosed conflict of interest is discovered.

Find out if the arbitrator has ever served in an arbitrator role before for the other party; some businesses use the same arbitrator, panel or firm over and over again, and you don't want an arbitrator who desires repeat business from the other party.

Ask about any previous relationships the arbitrator has had with the other party (or with the other party's attorney) or with any associates, family members or agents of these individuals in the past.

Don't be afraid to ask questions! Also ask for a signed document from the arbitrator disclosing any potential conflicts of interest or confirming no conflicts of interest.

What if the Arbitrator Demonstrates Bias or Misconduct?

Arbitrators must be neutral, which means they should never show bias towards either party. If you see evidence of bias, there is very little you will be able to do to stop the arbitration process; however, an award made by this arbitrator could be vacated if you can prove that bias or misconduct occurred—but this is difficult to prove.

It is best to try to prevent problems of bias or misconduct by . . .

. . . **using a panel of arbitrators (typically three arbitrators) who must confer and agree on an award (a decision) together. It is highly unlikely that an entire panel of arbitrators would have a conflict of interest in the case.**

. . . **making sure all arbitration hearings are recorded by a court stenographer. If you fail to do this, you will have no record of the hearing, which could be required by the courts in the future if you are trying to prove that bias or misconduct occurred in your case.**

. . . **selecting an arbitrator (or an arbitration panel) with extensive experience, credentials, training, knowledge in the area of law that pertains to your case, and references who can attest to the arbitrator's integrity and abilities.**

. . . **avoiding arbitration altogether by using a non-binding mediation process to retain control over your own conflict resolution.**

. . . **asking the arbitrator to disclose any conflicts of interest—as stated earlier in this book, it is critical to ask the arbitrator to sign a document verifying that he or she has no previous or current relationship with either party and that the arbitrator has no conflicts of interest with either party (or with their attorneys).**

For more information, read the following cases on the Internet: *Burlington Northern Railroad Company and the Atchison, Topeka & Santa Fe Railway Company* and *Petitioners v. Tuco Inc. and Southwestern Public Service Company No. 95-1317.* The courts stated: "We therefore hold that the disclosure standard we have articulated today likewise applies to conflicts arising during the course of the arbitration proceedings. Moreover, to preserve the integrity of the selection process, we hold that a party who could have vetoed the arbitrator at the time of selection may disqualify the arbitrator during the course of the proceedings based on a new conflict which might reasonably affect the arbitrator's impartiality. If this were not the rule, the control which the parties contracted for in the arbitration agreement would be undermined."

A Summary of Key Points About ADR

This book has been written to assist USA citizens without legal backgrounds to work more effectively with an attorney to resolve conflicts in the least expensive and least emotionally painful manner possible. My hope in writing this is that you will be "armed with information" to make good and proactive decisions, and that you and the other party can resolve your dispute quickly and effectively.

Here are a few final key points to remember:

- When you are in dispute with another party, it is a very emotional time—be aware of your high emotional state and don't let your emotions cause you to make poor decisions that you will regret later.

- Always remember how much a legal dispute could affect your family, your friendships, your job or business, and your financial situation, so keep asking yourself—*is this dispute really worth the stress? Can we resolve this together without incurring legal expenses?*

- Remember that currently there are no federal requirements for training, education, certifications, experience or any other credentials for a mediator or an arbitrator to "hang a shingle" and start this type of business. So you MUST ask potential mediators and arbitrators about their credentials and evaluate their qualifications.

- While most arbitrators are ethical, fair and knowledgeable, if you choose an arbitrator who is missing one or more of these traits you could be in trouble. This is because an arbitrator can make virtually any binding decision, and it is impossible for a court to change an arbitrator's award. A court can vacate (nullify) an award, but this is very rare. Choose an arbitrator with experience and high standards of integrity. Make sure the arbitrator will be an objective arbitrator for both parties. Choose an arbitrator who is knowledgeable in the area of law that pertains to your dispute. Choose an arbitrator who has enough available time to focus on your case.

- If you sign a contract with an arbitration clause, you are waiving your civil right (that you have paid for with your tax money) to use the public court system to resolve any dispute that may arise. Also, the other party can force you into arbitration even if you don't want to escalate the dispute (although if **both** parties agree, they can choose to attempt to settle the dispute in mediation first).

- You have the right to ask a contract owner to change an arbitration clause into a mediation clause in any contract you sign—this can either be typed in formally, or handwritten as a change with both parties signing their initials to this change. Check every contract for an arbitration clause **before** you sign it.

- If two parties can't resolve a dispute on their own, mediation is often the most effective and the least expensive way to resolve the dispute—both parties should be prepared to compromise in mediation, but the advantage is that the parties retain control over their own situation.

Additional ADR Information Resources

Helpful information is provided about arbitration, mediation and the *Federal Arbitration Act* on Wikipedia, including advantages and disadvantages of these services and several important case law examples.

You can also view helpful information provided by the non-profit organization: *The National Academy of Arbitrators* at **http://www.naarb.org/**, although it is important to know that this professional forum is not a governing authority over arbitration, nor is it an arbitration consumer protection group.

The Mediation Information and Resource Center at **www.mediation.com** is a good source of information about mediation services.

Be aware that other arbitration forums you can find on the Internet are usually businesses (providers of paid arbitration services) so their information will have a marketing slant and a goal of selling a service to you. However, these sites still provide very helpful information about arbitration. One helpful site is the American Arbitration Association at **www.adr.org** (this is a business and not a government entity).

Both mediation and arbitration procedures are affected by state laws. Conduct an internet search for helpful information by typing your state name followed by the words "mediation information" or "arbitration information" to find state law information, state ADR forums and ADR services in your area.

Glossary of ADR Terms

ADR—This acronym stands for **Alternative Dispute Resolution**, which refers to any process that is used outside of the public courtroom forum to resolve a dispute, such as negotiation, mediation, arbitration or any combination of these options.

Affidavit—This is a document containing voluntary statements made by a party under oath and signed under the witness of a legal authority, such as a notary public. The statements made by a person in an affidavit are considered to be equal to statements made by a person under oath in a courtroom; a person making false statements in an affidavit can be charged with perjury.

Arbitration—When two parties in dispute hire an individual (or a panel of multiple arbitrators) to hear their case and to make a binding decision to resolve their dispute, they are using the process of arbitration.

Arbitration Agreement—A contract created and signed by the parties in dispute (or created by an arbitration firm for the parties to review and sign) that governs the arbitration rules, procedures, timeline, requirements, and other terms of the arbitration.

Arbitration Clause—A statement in any legally binding contract which requires the parties who sign the contract to arbitrate any future disputes that may arise.

Arbitrator—An arbitrator is anyone who is hired to make a legally binding decision for two parties in conflict.

Award—The decision of an arbitrator is referred to as an award.

Award Confirmation—An award of an arbitrator is not a valid award until it is confirmed (approved) by a judge in a public court.

Award Vacatur—An award of an arbitrator can be vacated (dismissed) by a judge in a public court due to significant problems that occurred in the arbitration process. The *Federal Arbitration Act* details the narrow and specific types of issues that can be used to request vacatur of an arbitration award.

Code of Ethics for Arbitrators in Commercial Disputes—A document containing ethical guidelines and procedures for arbitrators to follow; this document was created by a joint committee of the *American Arbitration Association* and the *American Bar Association*.

Discovery—This process is used by parties in arbitration or in litigation to gather information from the other party, in the form of questions to be answered and/or in the form of documents or other items each party must provide to the other party.

Exhibits—Exhibits are documents and/or other items which are shown to a judge, to a jury and/or to an arbitrator to support the facts presented in the case.

Federal Arbitration Act (FAA)—The *Federal Arbitration Act* is Title 9, Section 1-14 of the *Code of Law of the United States of America*. This section of the US code contains the rules and procedures that govern arbitration at the federal level. State laws also exist which govern arbitration.

Hearing—A Hearing is held during litigation and during arbitration when a judge, and/or a jury, and/or an arbitrator hears information and testimony provided verbally and through exhibits to gather information that will be used to form a decision or award.

Interrogatories—This is a type of Discovery which requires a party to answer questions in written format and to provide these answers to the opposing party.

Litigation—This term is used to refer to any legal action taken by one party against another party.

Mediator—A mediator is hired by two parties to assist them in identifying ways to resolve their dispute(s). A mediator helps to create a less emotional and structured environment for the parties to create their own resolution ideas. The role of the mediator is not to make a legally binding decision for the parties, but to help the parties make their own decisions to end their conflict and to create a Mediated Settlement Agreement (MSA).

Model Standards of Conduct for Mediators—These standards were written in 1994 and revised in 2005 by a joint committee that included members of the *American Arbitration Association*, the *American Bar Association* and the *Association for Conflict Resolution*. Additionally, in 2005 the Supreme Court approved *Ethical Guidelines for Mediators*.

Motion—A procedure used to bring a legal issue to a public court of law. For example, after an arbitrator makes an award, the winning party will need to motion the court to confirm the award, and the losing party can submit a motion to vacate the award, if the grounds to vacate the award exist (the grounds to vacate an award are listed in the *Federal Arbitration Act*).

MSA—The abbreviation for **Mediated Settlement Agreement**, which is the legal document used by parties in mediation to document their own settlement terms. Once the parties both sign the MSA, it becomes a legally binding contract.

Neutral—Often a mediator or an arbitrator is referred to as a neutral. This means that mediators and arbitrators are required to serve in an objective role without any conflicts of interest and without personal bias or agendas that could affect their behaviors and/or their decisions.

Production Requests—A type of Discovery which requires a party to provide documents to the other party or to allow the other party to inspect documents, equipment and/or other items pertaining to the dispute.

Retainer—An amount of money you will pay up front to a legal firm, which will be placed into a bank account and drawn from as the firm works on your case.

Vacate—This term means to dismiss or to nullify. An arbitration award can be vacated by a court of law (although this occurs very rarely), but an arbitration award can never be changed or overturned by a court of law. When an arbitration award is vacated, it is as if the arbitration never took place and the arbitration award never existed, and the parties' conflict is not resolved.

Acknowledgements

First and foremost, I want to thank Duane for being by my side throughout my entire experience in alternative dispute resolution—for reminding me to breathe, for reminding me to keep everything in perspective, for being patient and for listening.

I also want to provide special thanks to my Dad for helping me through this process, for believing in me and supporting me.

To Spencer and Jeremy—I wish my experiences in arbitration had not impacted you for multiple years. I hope that by writing this book others will understand the impact of conflict and litigation on family members and that the information in this book will help others avoid the problems that impacted all of us.

Thanks go to Spencer, Eldon, Dale, Sue and Julie for reviewing, editing and proofreading this book, and to Jeremy for creating the original artwork for the cover of this book.

Thank you to all of my family members and friends for your support, your prayers and your understanding.

To Julie and Diana who assisted me in so many ways in the past few years—I thank you also for your friendship and support through this process.

Special thanks go to mediator and arbitrator Kathy Fragnoli and to Mike Costello for reviewing this book and providing feedback to enhance the book content and accuracy.